While Away

Poems by

Kevin Rabas, Linzi Garcia, Brett Seaton

Spartan
Press

Spartan Press

Kansas City, MO

spartanpresskc.com

Spartan
Press

Design, edits, and layout: Linzi Garcia

Kevin Rabas Author Photo: Dave Leiker

Linzi Garcia Author Photo: Dave Leiker

Brett Seaton Author Photo: Brett Seaton

Acknowledgments:

Thank you to Jason Ryberg and Spartan Press for your faith in this project. Thank you for helping to transform our separate journeys and the notes taken during those times away into something we can share more widely, turning experience and private tales into dialogue and public art.

Kevin would like to say, "Thanks to Lisa, as always."

TABLE OF CONTENTS

KEVIN RABAS

LINZI GARCIA

BRETT SEATON

INTRODUCTION

Emporia, Kansas, 23 March 2022

How someone lives while away can tell you a lot about them:
What's home? What's to return to, and what's to escape?
Where can you go? How long can you afford to be away?

These poems and writings grapple with these age-old
questions, along with a simpler one: Who am I, while away?

Enjoy the answers to these (and many more) questions
while reading. Also, enjoy the neo-Beat ride.

Linzi and Brett are both mentees of mine, and it is joy to
feature their work beside mine.

—Kevin Rabas, Poet Laureate of Kansas (2017-2019),
  More Than Words

A journey of a thousand miles begins with a single step.

– Lao Tzu

KEVIN RABAS

Poet Laureate of Kansas (2017-2019), **Kevin Rabas** teaches at Emporia State University, where he leads the poetry and playwriting tracks. He has sixteen books, including *Lisa's Flying Electric Piano,* a Kansas Notable Book and Nelson Poetry Book Award winner. Rabas is the winner of the Langston Hughes Award for Poetry, the Victor Contoski Poetry Award, the Jerome Johanning Playwriting Award, and the Salina New Voice Award.

[In 1034 pages of poetry drafts, Kevin Rabas uses the word travel 22 times]

Some part of it was being where it was at: LA, New York. The Beats drove miles, drove nights, to see each other, and to be in the scene. Could I do that? (Did I?) And what about me now?

***

That evening, I remembered how we sat on mats in your house without a/c, how we'd close our eyes and travel across town or across the solar system. At least this is what we thought we might be doing, and I didn't doubt it long. I just let it be. And when Z asked me to twist one leg around the other leg, while standing like a stork, it seemed like a thing anyone could do, until she said, "Good. I didn't think a tense, pent up guy like you could do it."

***

She was going on a trip, did not travel often, did not know how and what to pack.

***

It would be little different if I were rich. I would only sleep easier. (And travel.)

***

E asked me to ride w him when he drove around today, mainly to run errands, but also to talk, to have company. He's off today because the juniors take the ACT, and so there's no school for the others. It's a nice day. High of 70. I got him gas. And he's out there driving around by himself now, as I prepare for meetings, make calls, and have lunch. (I'm including a receipt from our travels, just for kicks. It shows where we went and when. A kind of record. I got a small box of seltzer water at Walgreens.)

***

[at the new school]

She had three watches on one arm and four on the other. He had never seen such a thing. Time travel must be her thing, he thought.

***

[TV and time travel in Marvel]

In *Loki*, the dark elves kill the trickster's mother, and, seeing that, he doesn't really want to go back.

***

And what can you do for your son, but listen, and help when you can? Some roads must be traveled alone.

***

[not long after the divorce]

Mark doesn't get to see / his little kids that often / anymore. I hope they know / he loves them. / He builds them clocks, / invents new ones, with unusual / movements, pendulums that not only / teeter, but spin. / Time is no longer something / they spend much of together, / but time is still / spent, ticked, / and like the light / that travels / from a lost, gone star, / we still see

it, shining, / even after that star / has passed back into blackness / and is gone.

***

He had traveled Eastern Europe alone, writing on little notepads along the way, hoping to find someone to one day share this journey with.

***

It had gotten bad. He might not travel like that again.

***

What she said with her bow on her cello was what the whales said, something that traveled far underwater, a language we might have once known, but forgot, when we fell in love with the sun.

***

Some traveled to the mountain or the beach with pencil and pen. He sat out front of his house. That was enough.

***

Using the page he could time travel, a little forward and a whole lot back.

***

how the ride is played
  with the left
on top the doom doom shell,
  back back back
from the ways it's played
  in Africa, that's how
the bright cowbell is hit,
  not backward,
but way way back,
  a kind of time
travel, played right.

***

Curtis: I'd like to try it, but I feel like I'd misuse time travel.

***

They wanted to play a game. Toss a ball. Hop and
score. I wanted to watch and read and write. Travel. Be.
Those sorts of things.

***

A lot of people
   at the Walmart
limp, can't stand
   too long, can't wait
to get out
   and into cars
and go, move
swift and sure and smooth,
   travel as if
they may never
   have to get out.

***

[humble front porch]

I really don't need / to travel, can sit / right here and
write.

***

That coffee bean traveled long and far to be crushed and
hot in your pot. Respect it. Drink it a little more slowly.

***

This music had traveled across an ocean…

***

Not too many

    rehearsals, and it sounds

like we've traveled

    back in time, the concert

set in some drafty castle.

    Hold my hand.

I'm dying.

[nyc then]

I.

You can go in under / the yellow "M" / and get an egg
between / two pieces of puckered bread, / lamp-heated,
cheap, / or you can stand in the street / while someone fries
one fresh, / battered spatula in hand, the steam / around
his head, halo-like, fresh.

II.

It was something, being a Kansan in New York. He was
visiting relatives for a few days. And it was so very different
here. Full of people, bustling. And everywhere there were
the arts, as if it were a part of breathing, taking something
beautiful in.

[nyc now]

I wonder what it's like in New York? Last time we were there, everyone was out, milling the sidewalks, no thought of the bug, no thought of whose breath is on the air— someone with the sickness, some monster death angel in the wind.

That evening, the piano comes through the phone, and it's another live-stream night, no one in the clubs, but we can sit at home in Emporia and feel we're in KC or NYC or anywhere the music is made, and a camera is set up, sending to us.

We may never again go to New York.

[and pack light]

There's something about the road, knowing you have to
have everything you need in one pack on your back.

[both on the road]

He worried about his son, the roadtrip he was
on, one of the kid's first. He'd taken his own
as a kid, was robbed and played music on the
street, enough to get back on the bus, get back
on the train.

[nobody's road]

Get too tired / and rub up against / the rumblestrip, /
and you'll be reminded: / this isn't some loose cruise, /
and this isn't / your own road.

[roadtrip, older, hotels]

It was a long drive, and he had taken it, going slowly, stopping when he wanted, spending the night.

Mountain Time Horizon

Although the state flag has them, purple, in the background, there are no mountains in Kansas, and so when we go to Yellowstone, we look for the skyline, but can't see it, and instead see rock up from the ground, like giant golem shoulders, like bison backs furred in green. There's no looking to the horizon. What you see is all in shadow. You're at the foot of mountains.

[Yellowstone]

You arrived
  in your car
  from the city,
and it was like
  commencement, how the hands
come together, how we
  hugged, as if a future
began that afternoon.

[Yellowstone, out of the car and
into the wilderness]

Most of the day
spent in the car, and we're out
on the walk over the water,
white steam, white smoke
around us, like stepping
from a dream
into waking, Yellowstone
we walk your dirt paths
and wooden boardwalks,
like people with parasols and woolen
suits once did, same place, same
view. You know something
special is here to see, to do.
You know the world does not
all look like this, does not bubble
and spout and blossom
with bison, with elk, with wolves,
but it once did.

[Yellowstone sketches]

Someone keeps throwing pennies into the hot pool into the lip of Morning Glory. How the park rangers want to kill him.

***

Beyond almost everything at Yellowstone are the trees—tall and green, standing tall and straight, as if watching. Be good, be careful, they say.

***

When we stop, we click pictures. There is nothing else like this.

***

How the air is cool and dry, morning in the mountains.

***

Lisa says breakfast is ready, and we spoon cereal to our lips in the parking lot.

***

Around everything there is a rail, not to keep it in, but to keep you out.

Little Alicia

J: When Alicia was out hiking by a lake, they saw a bear, and the bear jumped in the lake and swam across. The bear didn't want anything to do with them.

J: Back then you could bring picnic baskets into the park and coolers. And a bear came, walked right up with purpose, like he'd done this before, and Daddy started throwing cheese at him, and said get in the car, and we did, and the bear put his big paws up on Daddy's shoulders, and he threw some more cheese, and the bear went away.

[What are we all here for?]

How small they seem
on the boardwalk, the people
from other continents
come to see the geysers, the hot pools,
the bison and the wolves. Here
in Yellowstone every view
is a large one, long one, like looking
through a scope, there's something always
out there on the other end, small, a dot
at first, but furry, moving, when you zoom
in, and that's the way of it, walking
at the skirt of the wilderness, knowing
we're only visiting, don't live here, just come
to watch and walk and want
that kind of peace.

Singing Them Home

Let out of the metal trailers
   and back onto the land,
   the buffalo run
at top speed
   and don't stop, run
past the horizon line.
   I don't know
what they do
   once they
pass the sun. But
men with drums
   stand at the edges
and sing.

RE: video of Yellowstone, 23 Aug. 2019

When my mom stops the car, my dad gets out to piss,
sends a yellow stream in front of the Yellowstone,
long mottled river in front of a skirt of green trees,
lodgepoles. My father pisses with the urgency his
father once did coming back from the funeral. Can't
wait. Must piss. And the line of cars drive by in a row:
silver cars, blue cars, and the black hearse. And as they
go, they try to turn away.

[back when I had the cash and time to travel]

for Lisa

It's been three weeks,
and I've been to Yellowstone
   and NYC,
and now am back
   in KC
in its best coffeeshop,
and in she walks, the woman I love,
and overhead "the very thought
   of you" is on,
and it's easy, so very easy
to pull out a chair
   for her.

LINZI GARCIA

Linzi Garcia can be found frolicking through fields, cemeteries, bookstores, and bars across the states. Her full-length poetry collection, *Thank You*, was published in 2018 by Spartan Press, and her chapbook about studying abroad in London, *Live a Great Story* (co-written with Jase Buck), was published by Analog Submission Press (2019). While getting her MA in English at Emporia State University, Linzi worked as the graduate assistant to Poet Laureate Emeritus of Kansas Kevin Rabas and as an editorial assistant with Bluestem Press and *Flint Hills Review*. Linzi now serves as the publicist at Meadowlark Press and the poetry editor for its imprint, Meadowlark Poetry Press.

dream sequence #1

driving in the dark—
on and on and on and on—
convinced the sun will never rise again.

Waking up in a Love's Parking Lot

Tiny little frog faces all over the ground! So small, you would step on them if you were not looking. So small, they could not hop up the curb toward freedom. J leads a few into his hand at a time and catapults them (gently and with sound effects) over the fence that separates parking lot and lagoon. "I had to save them," he says. "They are the frogs that sang to us all night."

Under the Veranda

Outside of Jason Ryberg's
seasonal living quarters,
a child from years past wrote
Family ♥ on the stoop
under the veranda.

Being a Kansas transplant,
my family is far.
Ryberg's family lives
just a few blocks away,
but even that feels far
enough sometimes.

Here, we have
become family.

Exploring Omaha

I:
London pigeons
stay on the ground;
Omaha pigeons
stay in the sky—
I am always
in a room
in between.

II:
I have a car
but choose to walk,
smile at passersby.

III:
Omaha pigeons nest
in ornate condemned
theatre windowsills—
repurposed,
not wasted.

IV:
Naked marble lady
in that window over there,
I see you.

I fit my reflection
to your shape—
head down, back bent,
arms up, hands together,
reaching.

V:
Down the street from
the Will Brown memorial
plaque, stains of powerwashed
graffiti from riots
after George Floyd's death—
100 years since Brown's.

We haven't changed enough.

VI:
They see her
writing and walking,
tell her she's not
from here, not
like anyone here,
and she's not from here,
but she knows there are
others like her—
simple servants
out to make the most
of this precious life.

Flight A321, MCI→ATL

I'm in love
with the world from above—
we were too close
to the lines and shapes
to see it all
before.

Look!
The baseball diamonds
and their manicured lawns
are sand dollars
from up here!

Unlike other places,
we don't build along
Kansas rivers—untouched,
ungroomed, wild, and native.

All the little ponds scattered
across the prairie
catch the morning sun
and look like flakes of gold
leading me away from home.

No Nightmares at 20,000 Feet, Please

I am reminded
of *The Twilight Zone*
episode, where William Shatner
sees a monster
on the airplane wing,
though it appears
he's just crazy, and I pray
I see no such things
on the wing or in the cabin,
as these volatile times have
some of us crazed
and some of us monstrous.

Vacation

I would rather
think,
listen,
and if the
urge arises,
write,
than anything else.

Life

is

full.

Quiet

                        thinking,

listening,

                  writing

time

is a luxury.

Inspired in a Few Ways

I think of Kevin Rabas's
poem about flying to Yellowstone—
how the Rockies looked like
chocolate chip ice cream
with chocolate sauce drizzle.
He was flying the opposite
direction as I am now,
and all I can see
are cottage cheese clouds.

No Coast⟶Coast

The soft hill of the rolling wave
catches the moonlight, smoother than glass.
The beam does not stretch
with the perfect angle passing,
but cuts, its twinkle catching
traces of Atlantis.

Every Place Sounds Different

Home, you must listen for what's there—
birdsong, wind and bugs, a train in the distance.

Here, the ocean sings all the time.
The ocean sings all the time.

This close to the ocean,
this big of a moon,
I can feel the tide inside me.

An Air of Concern

The train's history is dark,
helpful, complex.
Powerlines, trains, and rivers—
the only things that cut
through this country
with no remorse,
opposition,
consideration,
or care for the land and its people.

Carrollton, MO

Our train passes through your town,
but I wouldn't know that without
the water tower.

I wave your direction,
to the junkyard dogs,
and to the ghost
who sits in the easychair
at the bottom of that driveway.

Uneasy

We ride past the remains
of a derailed freight train
and stare in silence.

What could have happened
for it to have burst from the inside out,
for its body to be so, so mangled?

You won't see…

16 bald eagles in one spot anywhere
else than the backside of Ft. Madison.
They crowd the lakemelt
for water and fish, and you can tell
they are tired and hope
winter will subside soon.

Business Travel

Tuesday night meetings
at cigar lounges, hookah
houses, and Irish pubs
make all Wednesday morning
professionals foggy, achy, yet ready
to present, network, go out again.

Drinks with the Rabbi

I.
The Rabbi walks
into a bar,
white suit—gold buttons
ready to burst—
matching cap,
matching tie,
purple slippers.

Adorned with a bouquet
of baby's breath & fern,
a boutonniere to match,
he tells the bartender
he's looking for the girl
with green eyes.

The Rabbi walks
into a bar
for me.

Me, an old 25.
Him, a young 76.

We drink beer &
talk about the time
& space that led us
here together.

II.

The Rabbi used to travel
the world, chasing girls, chasing
beaches. When the love ran
dry, there was always the water,
always the sunsets, always
the boats way out there,
coming & going as they do.

III.

The Rabbi was a military man,
son of a Navy man, climbed
the ranks to Lieutenant Colonel,
didn't bat an eyelash when he met
the late Herbert Hoover.

IV.

The Rabbi hides a toy fish
in his pocket, keeps it handy
to toss on the floor, stir
up laughter, when conversation lulls.

V.

The Rabbi says he keeps
a pocket printer on him too,
asks for a piece of paper.
He makes robotic noises
beep-beep, boop-boop,
scribbles his Jewish
name, his Catholic name,
& his cell phone number.

Travel Shorts

Some day,
these poems will be in a book,
and I wonder what
anyone else got
out of this flight.
***
What is that plant?
Back home, corn.
Out here, tobacco.
***
Picket fences stretch on in all directions.
No more barbed wire here. Grapes, not corn.
Farmland in Johnson County.
***
Outside the tent,
mushroom cluster.
What's died there?
***
I want to leave
a little energy
everywhere I go—
haunt every place
I've spent a little life.

BRETT SEATON

Brett Seaton was born and raised in Manhattan, Kansas. He graduated from Olathe West High School and now attends The Wharton School at the University of Pennsylvania. Brett previously started a now-defunct literary magazine called *Astra Magazine* which published Kevin Rabas's work alongside Rudy Francisco, Ted Kooser, and Huascar Medina. Brett has published poetry in the *American Library of Poetry*, *Kansas Voices*, and *Elementia*. He is currently editing a second solo poetry manuscript.

Curdling

rocks are the cheese to magma's milk. truly.
it's quite wonderful watching it flow
and curdle and churn
curdle another couple of times
ok maybe there isn't that much curdling, i just like the
    word curdle
curdle.
it helps me forget the sight of a living,
elemental wonder
a red river dying, living beneath the surface, and dying again
because it cannot live long in such a cold
environment.

the rocky shell covers the lava until red tears
disappear under, "i don't care"s shouted into
pillows

or whispered while avoiding eye contact
with the one who unplugged
herself from
my life

the sun makes sure of it
day in then day out,
red turns black
until i don't want to write about it anymore

i want to write about cheese and curdling
and Hawaii's sandy beaches but
i keep coming back
to the volcano

i'm summoning it now
because i couldn't before
because when someone
chooses nothing over you

you become nothing
and somehow that is worse than nothing
it's worse than not having had something
in the first place

i'm learning the piano.
i thought poetry was enough
to break the crust around magma
shouting angry lines across
plains of hawaiian rock
sprinting up the mountain
shouting at an ocean of black

i jump into the volcano, hoping at least the earth would
take me back but at the bottom
it is only black

so even poetry
where i say she and her at all times
to confuse myself of who i'm talking about
because i'm really not sure anymore

even poetry can't find the magma anymore
and i'm just as straight faced
as i was before diving into the volcano

even poetry can't stop me from falling in love
with every conversationalist

it can't stop me from borrowing money
to buy tickets to every night club
and tell myself it's an investment

just to go stand near the middle and move my
hands in a circle

hoping that someone will find my face or shirt
or dance moves attractive

hoping that people care most about the crust
that surrounds my magma because
that's why I am here

poetry can't stop me
from searching faces in a night club
to find the next charge for my dead battery

yes
night clubs are in the business of hope.

so, i'm learning the piano
and every time i sit down

i brush my hands along
the plastic painted
to look like wood

i raise the covering
and i poke out one
note, wait
and another, wait
and wait again
SO I DON'T ERUPT

so i don't erupt
no, so I don't crack
and break
and get black
all over the pretty
little
piano
pieces

Runaway

Soon I must leave again
because that is the only power
love can't take from me

Idiots need God
to blame wrong on
I am an idiot

When I'm happy I romanticize the road
I total my own heart for the insurance money
which I end up spending on bandages

Then the pain comes
and God turns my heart
into TV static

Freedom is sweet
after time, it ferments
I'm drunk from loneliness

Walking home on a sidewalk
leaves fall and block my way
they crunch when I shuffle forward

Children play in golden sandboxes
their parents taking careful notes
trying to remember happiness

John and Josie share a toy car
a look, a drink, a diamond ring
while a plane sits on the runway

Towns with dirt roads
cities with street lights
matchmakers all

This is love I want to say
this is love I want to stay
this is love I'll run away

Vacation

I moved to Costa Rica two weeks ago
and in two weeks I will move back

I just finished hemingway's a farewell to arms
the main character's wife and child die
in the last two pages of a 350 page book

when the drip pan is 7 billion people deep
the pain is unbearable at the bottom

so our human life dies down to its root.

the beach is not a cliché

it breathes satisfaction, it births mist
into the air, washing over its
audience in waves

the sun on the surface of the ocean is a walkway to heaven
which means that
heaven might not be above us after all

just, if we take this path
press our hands together, our lips to dirt
white pillars will be there
on the other side of the horizon

it is the stairway to heaven
descended to earth

and hammered flat onto the up and down watery infinity
rays extend to me
hello,
as the sun falls

it falls slowly, so slowly
then all at once to the horizon because

it doesn't care like the wind
it is just a morning star.

the ocean didn't used to exhale

it meant exploration, fear
it meant inaudible inhale

it meant is there an is there
beyond this place?

blue was the color of these things,
there was more day to dawn

today, blue is a color of
airline attendant's aprons
pushing drinks, crackers and sleeping pills

natives play non-native music
for non-natives to relax
while confusing non-nativity with tourism
while confusing similarity with ownership

a lone mariachi strums a minor note
for the moon
but when the sun rises
he plays another party song

burning, a tree by the estuary falls into it
the ocean boils
then the current carries ashes
to sea

the audience cheers
they clap each other on the back
gamblers groan, some grin on lawn chairs, take a
sip, money changes hands

water is the same here
and everyone relaxes.

holes in maps are getting bigger
every one of the birds
has gone back to their nests, that they have seen
the sky

from their perch, birds see
a little palm-dock
with someone's grandfather's flag
planted in the wood

o, tree, light up for me
blaze unendingly: your soldier now and always
against the world's ordinaries

they graze, they're sheared,
they're slaughtered

shh shh don't talk about that while
the sun is setting

yes,
light up a distant island's silhouette
you look so close
islands are loud against the quiet waves.

the waves are flat here

the ocean should have topography
it should have mountains from which the sharks
can swim
downward as the lion pounces
downward as the billionaire corkscrews
downward
like snowflakes to the valley

mountains are on my left and right
I sit in the middle of a cove, the bottom of a
valley
I eat cake

now I see, a mile out at sea, a wave swell, crest,
crash,
and collapse back
to the million little ice cream licks surface

the sun is five feet
four feet 6 inches
four feet
from the island that it will set on to my eyes

which is miles

it has warmed a distance around it
and lighted a path to the beach that seems to
steam
expanding endlessly within itself.

my father told me to write simply

that, like hemingway, short sentences make the
writer
but I don't listen to anybody
older than me

here is life
but it does not avail to me
that they have tried it

the stars are dim tonight
angry streetlights roar
and still break the darkness with
what wonderful little pillars

I don't want to be happy
I aim to be very unhappy in life
it is a goal of mine

waiter, pour a long island iced tea.

the sun will go behind clouds now

a kayak rows itself uneventfully half a mile from
the beach
a black and white pelican jumps once
and glides to a buoy

I look again at the empty
water glass and the stained
espresso cup on my table

forgive me, children, for I have sinned
I have been thinking about the future
again

real children are difficult
as the kayak can attest to, who needs them?

it would be a warm life
people are too selfish: those who don't know what
hedonism is are hedonists
as the scripture says:
they shall masturbate infinitely onto their chests.

pessimism, depression
these are the lowest forms of expression

like a salesman's extravagant plumage
it is nothing

the butterfly flits among the palm trees
waves roll over and fall asleep
on burnished sand
I know the waves are still awake
and that butterflies don't flit
they fly

contradictions are the fire of life
I choose to burn, burn, burn.

palm leaves dominate the skyline
they filter clouds, sunlight, horizon, water

and a little white sailboat
anchored 30 rods offshore

the sun is lower

a slice is below the clouds that capture it
sunnyside down egg
with yolk running down to the water

blue dancers twirl
and rock over my vision when I look away
that's ok

drip pans and eyes can agree on this:
life is too short not to stare at suns

lovers, loners:
all the world watch it fall.

and still falling
only a foot or two from the ocean now

bugs bite my legs and flutter nervously
the sun is a perfect circle
please stare

she turns and she turns
burns and she burns into my eyes

so I can carry her forward
chisel her profile onto my chest
murder it into fertile women
to write the elegy of a generation
in its killer's milk.

orange touches the horizon
I am a tourist

pictures replace memory but I don't blame
the fallen
I mine the beam from my eye
lick ink from the pen
and brush motes from the camera

thou shalt not release perfection unwittingly
into the masses

who, unprepared,
break into shards
of alabaster egg shell

blown from the lungs of god
into the cosmos:

the sun has ruined sex.

color drains
the night grows, and drops into a khaki bathtub

my drink hasn't come
here, take some drugs while the wheel runs
close your eyes and
watch the spokes roll forward

now, look at the pool bar
drunk suburban wives
are my favorite reminder that life
could be worse

in their defense, it isn't their fault that
staircases
abandon the
fallen

the christians must write
some new shit
when the sun explodes

the waiter is upset
that I scattered pills
around my feet

while the sky has waxed warmer again.

when I consider warmth
I know
my great grandchildren will be nothing like me

heirlooms, childhood
nurture, nature
if every empire crumbles,

imagine
what will become
of me.

purple dies and black is born
night is darkest in light of beauty

I haven't learned anything
God wasted his breath

here I am
another day farther from birth
another day closer to death.

Song of Songs

Sing a tune to me
Sing a tune, my love
I'm here for the day
Then I'll go away

I want to boil this city
And pour it down my throat
So, when I'm away
My home will keep me warm

Come hold onto me
Come hold on my love
There is only today
Before the night is here to stay

No one knows my name
And who I am, I don't know
But time's too short for knowing
It's time to go

Come touch the sea
Come touch the sea my love
Hike the craggy peaks
And corner the earth with your eyes

Quit your job
Come see the world my love

You can't see the sunset
From a skyscraper

From Serengeti to Sicily
Shanghai to Switzerland
Let's go somewhere we haven't been
Sing along and come with me.

Shadow

I leave her at a deserted gas station
slip back to the driver's seat
and race off into the dark
I watch in the rearview mirror
as your silhouette dissolves in a dust cloud

The engine hums beneath me
my steady hand rolls down the windows
I shout defiance into the open sky
rider-less horses run on the freeway
soon they tire and quietly fade away

I drive until the fuel tank fails
my armor falls off piece by piece
until only the knight remains
stepping out onto sand dunes
I search for my castle

my feet slide beneath
a blanket of grain
I am so tired
but I keep
I keep climbing

I keep climbing over hills
over hills and valleys
I keep climbing

the sand sinks
the burned ruins
of my old home

the ruins of my home
the skeleton and visceral
I am so tired

I rest among the ashes
I am tired, I rest in the ashes
so cold the death of flame

Diary

Driving on the way from Lander, WY to Jackson, WY
    to see the Tetons.
Last night my friends Kevin, Nathan, and I
stayed in a cabin
on an island in the middle of a river
its arms reuniting outside the window in burbling rushes. Snow sprinkles
from ice-dusted branches spiraling into the heavens.

Yesterday we stayed in Denver.
The downtown there feels like bootleg Boston
a western, intellectual, weed-filled city
saturated with Appalachian dread locks:
too many skateboards, patagonias, and flannel shirts.

We have chicken thigh sandwiches while climbing the red rocks amphitheater
and then sprint off into the Wyoming night.
It is a lonesome, empty kind of night
filled with stars so bright that you realize the sky
is all stars—full of stars—only obscured to darkness
by clouds of efficiency that hang so thickly in the cities
that you can taste the cottony flavor of oblivion.

An oblivion that turns continents
and cultures so diverse
you could spend a lifetime exploring
…into the city in front of you… blurred at the edges…

an eternal cloudy day that folds future and past
into chains of the present... an oblivion of ignorance...
the oblivion of necessity.

Everything feels like nothing, approaching the
end of the world
the edge that one could fall off of as easily
as a leaf twirling to the ground

only when it is cold, the earth is flat
and the expanses brush your skin with its
barrenness.

Wyoming is this way.
Not till we have lost the world do we begin to
find ourselves
and realize where we are
and the infinite extent of our relations.

It is dark and quiet and a soft wind tickles the
hair on my arms.
Grass husks pushed flat by the weight of the sky
fills all edges of sight:
captaining rocky hills and ridges into the oceanic
darkness, the waters
bumpy up and down and up again,
skating over red rocks, gray-green mounds, and
white caps of stone alike
before the wind slows, the seed drops,
and the river runs forward.
We stop at a camping site on the edge of a half-
frozen river.

The edges are gilded in ice.
I slip on the way down the river's edge
poking myself full of burrs and crushed berries.
We make our way out onto the ice jutting
across the rapids.

Winter is a marbled symphony
and every snowflake, every bear
sings a different strand of the tapestry
I run, jump, and land
on the other side of the river.
Man is at root destructive.
My feet tunnel through years of ice crystals
locked in tango
growing to the beat of rain and sun,
light brushes of rabbit paws scurrying across the
alien surface.
Then gone like all things.

I want to go too.
I want to go away from home
and jump into the waiting arms of adventure
into unimportant trajectories that push me
stumbling,
into the mischief of the world's greatest one-offs
and stories
to places uncorrupted by order and success.

Where life is measured in memories
not the power or wealth or recognition
you've paid for in stress and unhappiness.

I want to be remembered.

But I want to remember
life is a temporary position
a day trade that will be sold back before the
market closes.
The market always closes.

Closes in on me, memory, on life's virgin doe
in the bush, shot and grilled up for profit.
I want to live life at 40, at 30, earlier than most
when I still have freedom in my heart
and hunger in my gut.

It's disgusting, my bicameral mind.
I say this and yet, at best
I'll spend the best years of my life
paying into the pot of creation.

Why? To have my 40's and beyond free to live.
Must travel be glorious?
Can it not be simple and sustained?
I will answer this question
before I step into the pigeonholing of Economy.

To adventure when young and poor
or old and rich?

This is the question that the young must answer
with advice from the old

who are too embarrassed
to admit their regrets or too sold
on the rigidity of life's suggestions.

Shards of ice, my boots on the river's glass,
rainbows jumping from one beam of energy
to the next, to the next, and on.
Wyoming, man.

I collect snow in my arms
for the cooler in the car
I see the gouged earth

where I slipped
on the way down.
I repack the cooler.

I buckle back in.
I don't let the light
burn down my harvest.

www.ingramcontent.com/pod-product-compliance
Lightning Source LLC
Chambersburg PA
CBHW031247120626
46545CB00007B/2690